HEARTBREAK AND SLEEPLESS NIGHTS

MAHARANI SIRRIS

BookLeaf Publishing

India | USA | UK

Presentation by *BookLeaf Publishing*

Web: www.bookleafpub.com

E-mail: info@bookleafpub.com

ISBN: 9789360946586

First edition 2024

to the people I love
you know who you are

we cannot let other people's
approval be the condition as to
whether or not we are worthy
of being ourselves

heartbreak and sleepless nights

open your eyes
what do you see?
is the light shining in?
do you feel free?

are your emotions intact?
or do they run wild?
do they cause pain?
or do they make you smile?

what do you feel
when no one is looking?
do you feel lonely?
is it off putting?

is the silence loud?
or is it deafening?
or does the silent sound
feel comforting?

you spend too much time in your head
just as much time as you spend in bed
hop up, let's go somewhere instead

i am not saying it gets better
but we can have a cry
who knows it might make you feel better
it is worth a try

let the tears drop
let them roll
it is okay to feel sad
it is okay to lose control

as the sun rises
and as it sets
please tell me when you need a friend

This is Heartbreak and Sleepless Nights

HEARTBREAK

milk

we turned sour,
like off dated milk
or the can of beans in the corner of your
cupboard
that you intended to eat
but forgot about

we turned sour,
like the sleepless nights
and the blame game
between you and i

the worst part of this is
we intended to eat the beans
we would have put on the toast

we intended to turn the milk
into hot chocolate
as it was your favourite drink

but we turned sour
before we were able to try

bread crumbing

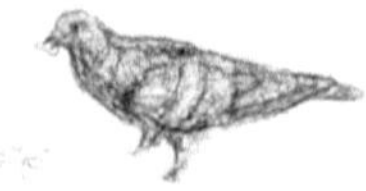

I grasp onto you, because you lay bread crumbs
and I am starving

I grasp onto you, because in my mind you are
the closest thing in my life to stability.

I grasp onto you, because I can not seem to make
sense of your words and actions

I grasp onto you, because you are so inconsistent that I
have no clue when or if you will show up

I have to remind myself that I am not starving
and I have to remind myself that you are not
stability
I have to remind myself you are not worth making
sense of
and I have to remind myself that there are other
people in my life that are consistent

but right now, you are a person feeding a hungry
pigeon and I am nothing but a wild bird to you

terrible

terrible at keeping relationships
terrible at keeping friends
terrible at loving people
it is all dead ends

i wait for you to show up
i wait for you to call
i wait for you to say you love me
even if you do not mean it at all

delusion

i sacrificed sleeping in my own bed,
because i thought sleeping in yours was
better
i sacrificed sleeping in my own bed,
because i thought having you near would
help take all the anger out of me

and i sacrificed sleeping in my own bed,
because i am delusional
in my head you are sleeping so close,
but in reality –
*you are at home sleeping in bed with
someone
who is not me*

learning silence

i stopped myself from saying any more,
cause you did not see the importance of
saying anything at all

what about these feelings i have got?

i don't know if you knew
what you were doing to my heart
maybe you were innocent

and did it out of courtesy,
and maybe i read it wrong,
and maybe you were being nice

but i am telling you
the way you touch my heart
and give it a warm hug
you knew,
you knew it would have made me fall in love
with you

what about these feelings i have got?
who is going to love me if it is not you?
who is going to care for me if it is not you?

but again,
maybe i am wrong,
and your heart belongs to someone else
that is not me

maybe she makes you coffee,
and adds the right amount of sugar
maybe she irons your clothes,
and folds your socks
maybe she is the one you go to after a hard
day of work

maybe she touches your heart,
and gives it a warm hug
maybe my feelings do not matter at all
and she is all you want

but, what about these feelings i have got?

longing

i long for your presence
i wait at the door,
like a wife waiting for her husband to come
back from war
i wait and wait for you to show up
but as time passes

i do not think you are coming at all

yellow sweater

i saw you walking today
in a yellow sweater
the one you always wear
i was startled, yet deep down
i knew you would not care

i looked and waited to see if you
would say something
nothing.
you ignored me
and i pretended not to care

a simple exchange from me to you
may seem nothing at the time
but my oh my. i have been thinking about it
all the god damn time

at work, between my shifts
between each camera
and each conversation with a customer
and at home to the ceiling,
to the wall.
to my pillow

to the imaginary you i see in my room,
and to everyone,
everywhere

i will make sure to say hi
even if you do not
because please know i was not ready to say
goodbye

let me tell you something funny,
but remember not to laugh
last year you were my reason to stay clean,
now you are the reason why i fall apart

times have changed
i struggle to remember your name
i am not kidding
i bet you feel the same

everything is better than missing you

i don't walk past your
favourite bubble tea store after work
because everything is better than missing
you

i don't order a flat white before work
because everything is better than missing
you

i catch the other train
and walk home in the rain
because everything is better than missing
you

i avoid wearing blue
even if it is my favourite colour

*because every other colour is better than
missing you*

clear as day

you believed in me
when no one did
you held my hand in the dark
until i was brave enough to make my own
mark

but, why did you give up?
why did you give up on me
at the end of it?

you let go of my hand
too quickly,
and i was left speechless
crying for days on end,
until i could no longer cry

what did i ever do to you?
what did i ever do to you?
to make you leave the way you did?

now you walk past me with no smile
i guess i was just another case file
did this not mean enough to you?

you went on and on about boundaries
do not worry i get it

it is okay,
i heard you clear as day

14

wanting what did not want you

i waited for it excitedly
i ran home from work
it was all i could think about

i clutched it in my hands
treating it like i was giving you a warm
embrace

i flicked through,
reading your letters to your so-called
past lovers
only realising i was there too

stomach drops,
swarming with guilt and memories
that i was not good enough for you
i pushed you away,
but i never meant to

as you say
you ended up wanting what did not want
you
so even in the end when she did not want
you, i still did

idea of you

i fell in love with the idea of you
the idea of us
being more than a few
smiles and hellos

being more than pleasantries
we shared
as we walked past each other
in the halls

and i fell in love with the idea of chasing
you,
and running after you
so it was me you would look at

but it became complicated
and i became tired
tired of the idea
that we would work
when i already knew we would not

and i fell out of the idea
of loving you
and i fell out of the idea of loving us

crazy over you

i am here going crazy
because this is not where i wanted to meet
you

i am going crazy because i have to love you
from a distance
a distance that cannot be reached by a car or
a bus or by a plane
it is an emotional distance between you and
i
for the best, of course
but that does not stop me from going crazy
over
you

obsession

i have an obsession,
it is not your typical obsession
like collecting things,
eating a certain food,
or an obsession you have a with a pop star

it is an obsession with finding people,
that look too close to my parents
an obsession in finding love and care in the,
wrong people

an obsession with finding a home within
people who already have a house
that is fully furnished
and always lit,
with scented candles,
and books,
and paintings

an obsession with finding people
that i know are emotionally unavailable
so i do not get hurt

but when that does not work,
time and time again
i always get hurt

break me first

i write you letters,
but never send them

letting you know how i am
and how my world is
but i do not think you would care

maybe i should be putting more effort
into my present relationships
because you are long gone,
i cannot reach you

but something about you,
keeps me holding on to the past
and wondering

if you did have the chance
to sit in front of me
whatever you say
i would eat it up

you have made me upset before
there is nothing to top that
i continue to put myself into those situations
because why the fuck not

i would rather live with that small
breadcrumb of you
than nothing at all

so i constantly poke at the wound
hoping the next time you see me

you would dress it,
you would kiss it better,
even if you broke me first

her and me

you were not here today
and i really wish you were
right next to me

but instead you are everywhere
in bookstores
on the streets

in my favourite bite to eat
in the walls
on the floor
in her arms

replaying the conversation we had yesterday
as she asks about your day

i get it
and i am not her
and i will never be

so spare my heart
as it is already broken in pieces
spare my tears
because i can't stop them

and tell me
the next time
you see me
the truth that lies beneath you

*what are we
and what am i to you?*

insanity

i get too excited when i hear your name
and my heart starts doing backflips

gosh, i feel like i am going insane

uncommitted relationship?

i talk about you to my parents
more than i should
making it look like we are in a committed
relationship

when we are not even friends
or colleagues, or classmates, acquaintances
or whatever you want to call it

when we only know each other by our first
names and favourite colours
maybe in an alternate universe
i will actually know you
and you will actually know me

know more than favourite colours
and small chats
and first names
maybe i will have a chance of reciprocated
love instead of
one sided

but bring me back to earth
and for now my parents know you as
someone who has a big heart
and i have accepted that it is enough for
now

me

25

i admit that i am jealous of someone i don't
even know
and i admit if you were not with her
i would pray that you choose me instead
despite the gap
or our different interests
i hope you choose me in another
universe

as i would
always choose you

the one

maybe you are not the one
and maybe that is why it is painful right now
because i am trying to make something
work
that is not supposed to

and maybe i will never understand why
and maybe i will always cry

but the only thing i can do now
is hope you land in the hands
of the right person
and that they will make you

as happy
as you make me

i have given up on chasing you,
or tearing her down
i have given up on thinking about you,
my head is spinning 'round and 'round

about you

the feeling was so intense
i thought it would never end
distracting myself;
making playlists

because i could not tell you how it felt
to love someone so deeply
that it hurt every part of my body

i could not stop crying
but no tears came out
and i felt numb just
thinking about you

no sleep, nothing but you on my mind
made me want to hide
and never see you again

because you would not get it
you would not understand

cause you have someone that loves you
and because i do not

but i guarantee
no one will love you like i do

fuck you, instead of thank you

why is it that you are destined
to be with her instead of me?
why did we cross paths?

especially, in the way that we did
was i not good enough for you
was i not good enough to be that close to
you

the universe deserves a fuck you,
instead of a thank you
for putting you in my life like this

so close, yet, so far from each other

where are you

i do not know where you are right now
probably at theirs,
sitting on the couch,
recalling your day

while i am sitting here,
not feeling okay

not the person

i need you terribly,
i crave your love and attention
but i also understand

you are not the person
that will give it to me

blurred boundaries

blurred boundaries
between you and i
but i cannot help but gravitate towards you
because you are everything my parents
aren't

blurred boundaries
between you and i
i should not feel this anxious and excited
around you
after all you are you,
and i am me

blurred boundaries
between you and i
we are in the red zone
but i like the colour red

so stay close,
close enough to keep us safe
and out of trouble

but far away,
so i do not get comfortable
with how you are treating me

*so i remember that i am just another
person to you*

mean it

sometimes i wonder what went wrong
what did i do to make you walk away?
what did i do to change your mind?
from "i will be here, right where you left me"
to "i am leaving you, goodbye"

was i that bad?
was i that bad of a person
for you to pick up and leave
when it was not convenient for you
anymore?

you said what you needed to say
but i held back
i held back because i
was scared to break your heart
cause in the end

i did not mean it,
but you did

you meant it

will you be like the rest?
tucked away never to be addressed
again
when the obsession with you is over,
and all i need is closure

dont feel right

it don't feel right
thinking of you
when you think of her

and it don't feel right
writing you letters
while you send her texts

and it don't feel right
pouring my heart out
while you get a paycheck

it don't feel right

*and maybe it never will
doing things for you,
while you only think about her*

goodnight, going to bed

please leave me alone
stop being nice to me
stop looking at me with those eyes
i no longer want it

i am going crazy
staring at your picture, wishing that it was
me
i am begging you
please walk out first
because i cannot find the strength to do so

gosh, get out of my head
goodnight, i am going to bed

consistency and reliability

you say you are consistent
in your actions
but i would say otherwise

you say that you are the same person
every day
but why is it
on some days i can lookdirectly at you
and others i am stood still looking at a
ghost,
wondering what kind of person i am talking
to

you say you are reliable
and that i can lean on you
but you do not show up when i need you the
most

consistency and reliability,
are just meaningless words to you

because at the end of the day
it is not real
fake promises is what you are

how it felt

i would not be able to tell you
how it felt
when you called for the last time
and said you are mine
i am speechless all the time

my stomach dropped,
and you were no longer a part of my life
wednesdays and tuesdays and fridays
became days
where i continued to live on

and so did you,
seeing me in the people you see everyday

she is all you need

i listen to songs you like,
eat the foods you eat,
become interested in the things you like
hoping all of this will pay off
and i will be all you need

but listening to the songs you like,
eating the foods you eat and *being
interested in the things you like
did not pay off
she's still   all you need*

missing you

there are moments in my day
where missing you holds me bed-bound
it locks my arms and legs in place
unable to move an inch

missing you is like pinning myself to the
sheets
because it is the place where i feel closest to
you

but i am unable to breathe

missing you takes all the energy out of me

dont you see?

long way

i walk the long way again today
past your office;
missing the train

it would be worth it if i saw you
i walk that extra mile
sweat dripping down my back

i should stop
because you are never there

and you never cared
about me

getting over you

i need to get over you
you cause me so much stress
and trouble
while you lay in their arms
i am doing every skill in the book to stay
calm

i am doing everything i can
so i do not start punching walls
or the floors
or the fucking tree outside my door

i am doing everything to stay afloat
not to drown in the abyss that i have created
for myself

i am doing everything i can to stay afloat
to not drown in all these tears
i spent crying over you

oh universe, give me ease
give me ease and let me accept what is
in front of me
that you spend your time with them

oh universe, let me get over you
because i do not want to be in this constant
agony
crying over you

just this once
let me rest
let me accept
let me be happy for you

let me be happy for me
let me love you from afar
that is all
i ask

furniture shopping

i went furniture shopping
looked at couches
and beds
and dressers
and wardrobes
and everything i think you will like
for our house that will never be ours

instead you are at yours and i am at mine
because we are not together
and never will be

sacrifices

i sacrifice
my values
my interests
and my happiness
to fit into the mould
you have created for me

i strip myself of everything that makes me
in hopes that you will finally see
that i am here
with open arms
waiting for you to fall into them

when they make you sad
and push you away
and want nothing to do with you

i am still in the mould
hoping you would take the time to look
at the perfectly curated version of myself
that suits to your liking

but you never looked
and i wasted my time
i no longer feel like me
but a me that is seen by you

i have wasted my time
just for you *to not even*
bat an eye
at
me

we walked past each other
like we had never met before

47

forgiven

i forgive you
i forgive you for all the miscommunication
we have had
i forgive you for all the times you did not do
anything when i came to you crying
screaming "I can not do this anymore"

i forgive you for all the times you made me
feel like shit
and for the times you sent me home when i
told you i wanted to kill myself

i forgive you for every single mean thing you
have done to me
i forgive you for the days you were so good
at your job it made me attached to you

i forgive you for reading my mind but never
seeing through me
and i forgive you for ending our one year
relationship with a
sixteen minute phone call

i forgive you for not stopping to say hi when
i walked past you

*i fucking forgive you, even though it rips
me apart
but tell me, what did i do to deserve this*

what if

what if it is always you
and i never move on

what if it is always you
no matter how many other people try

what if it is always you
the only person my love reaches

what if it is always you

i am never giving anyone a try
because it is always you

favourite person

i wait for you everyday
in the same spot
it is stupid
and pathetic
you do not even care about me

so what am i getting out of this
if you do not care about me

why am i waiting for you
like you are my owner giving me food
i am not starving
i have enough food on my plate

but still,
just around you
i suddenly have not eaten for days

and i crave all of you
suddenly i am hungry for your love and
attention
suddenly i cannot live without you

it is pathetic,
i am pathetic
to put all this on you

but i cannot help it
it is my bpd
craving all these things

all these things my parents never gave me

what if this is it for now

i fought to keep you
keep you near
for at least another year

cause i love you
more than you can imagine
but i lost you
just as fast as i got you

so i sit here
in tears
my heart is broken

that you are not near
and i tell myself
what if this is it for now?

coffee

you arrived first
when it was i who made the plan
i walked in touched you by the waist
while you waited for your drink

i ordered the cheapest drink on the menu
and sat down with you
rage filled my body

i looked everywhere but at you
i felt guilty
but i wanted nothing to do with you at the
same time

i wanted to tell you we were done
but nothing came out
you caressed my hands while holding them

i began to cry
the coffee became cold
even if it was iced

i could not do it
i could not let you go

it was impossible
all i could do was stare at my feet

mean

you are probably doing better than i am
you probably go out
have a ton of friends

a partner that loves you
i wish you well, truly
but you did not have to destroy me
to get ahead

you did not have to step on my heart
tear me to shreds
to find out that i was not the one for you
that was very mean of you

souls

it is okay if i cannot have you now
it is enough knowing that our souls
intertwined
in a past life

shadow

i saw you again today
i followed quietly behind
hoping you would just turn around
and say hi

but what happened,
realistically,
i followed you all the way to your office
sweat dripping, huffing and puffing
for a chance to talk to you

i got too nervous
i stopped in my tracks
watching your silhouette grow smaller and
smaller
until it was non-existent
it looked like something from a movie scene

i knew then you are not worth all of this
but something in me would not stop,
cannot stop running after you

searching for you in places you have
mentioned
in the drinks you drink
in the food you eat
the places you go

oh, i am so fucking miserable
don't you know

october

i hate you
i hate you so much
rage fills my body with your slightest touch

you cut deeper when i was still bleeding
i just want to scream at you
i want to shout at you

just so you know
that you put me in so much pain
it hurt every single part of my body

but maybe i am reading too much into this
and maybe you were not that mean at all

maybe you were the nicest person that i
have ever met
that did not make me feel small

and you took care of the cuts
instead of letting them bleed
helping me when in need

you gave me advice
instead of leaving me in the dark
holding a light instead of a spark

or maybe you did leave me in the dark
i don't know
i don't know the real you

and maybe i never will
but that is hard for me to accept
because i spent months talking to you

while you get a paycheck
i have spent months
cursing you

because it is easier to blame someone else
than to blame yourself

but it is done
and it is over
in the middle of october

maybe i still do

you lied to me
you said you would never leave me
i said one thing

that i am still regretting for the rest of my
life
you left me for the person you told me not to
worry about
and maybe i should have been a little more
cautious

but i trusted you
because i loved you
and maybe i still do

embarrassing

i talk about you a lot
i sit here on the floor writing poems about
you
hoping you never see them
because that is embarrassing,
my love for you is embarrassing

i sit here listening to all the songs you like,
but never singing them in front of you

because that is embarrassing,
my love for you is embarrassing

disagreement

this is getting exhausting
chasing the idea
that you will come back
when you are so long gone
that i am a stranger to you

but please
the next time you see me
remember all the times
we spent together

the laughter
the frustration
we shared

those winter afternoons
in my school uniform
and our puffer jackets

the summer mornings
with my rolled up sleeves
and your flowy shirts

oh, to go back to those times
i felt safe enough
to cry in front of you

do you remember those times
like i do
or did you erase all that when i left

did this mean as much to you
as it meant for me
no, i think you would disagree

bangs

65

i cut my bangs last night on the bathroom
floor
maybe you would like me more
if i looked like the person you have loved
before

snip, snip, snip
hair falls
i do not know who i am anymore

memo

you left me
without notice
without security
and i trusted you
to treat me right

it has been a year
you cannot just disappear
and leave me stranded
i felt so abandoned
wondering what on earth is wrong with me

it is me, is it not?
i am the problem

i thought so,
do not worry
i got the memo

my fault

i am embarrassed
i am crying to random people
whoever i can reach first

telling them everything about you
when they know nothing about me

defending you
while breaking me
so they know that this

*was all my fault
that you would never do anything to hurt
me*

when you say sorry, mom
you are supposed to mean it

i prayed that you would call
even though i knew you would not
i prayed you would stay
now i pray you will go away

today i woke up curled up in a ball
wishing the nightmares of you would
disappear

a years difference,
and there is nothing more left to say

though i do wish there was another way
to make you stay
i wish we had more time
maybe until next may

leaves have fallen off the trees
and you have left me
all alone
crying on my knees

you will be okay

i feel stupid
catching the train
and missing you

hoping i would see you at the next stop
even when i know i will not
even when i know in my heart
we are better apart

but how do i tell me -
the me that wants all of you
how to i tell her it is over
and there is no use wishing on a four leaf
clover

but it is okay,
as the sun sets
and as it rises

you will be okay
all of you will be okay

in a constant state
of trying to calm
    down.

it didnt end well

i dont care   youre cold as ice
out i do.   not even a smile
                        on your face
im complex
theres too   are you okay
many things   you wouldnt tell
going in!!   me anyways.
you went on 2 on
about boundaries
    dont worry i get it   you went on 2 on
    it's OKAY i heard you   about boundaries
        clear as day
when you say sorry mom!   dont worry i get
youre supposed to mean   it
            it.   it's okay, i heard
        i feel uneasy.   you clear as day.
keep going because i dont   change of heart
nt my professor to tell me i have
come back next semester.   i stare into every
                            cafe i walk past
furniture shop   desperately searching
ooking at couches   for anyone that
nd beds   Better?   looks like you.
and dressers   i'll die
nd wardrobes   anyway.
nd everything i think   empty stomach
ruly like   broken heart
                                    how did this
                                        all start?
or our house that   what about
ever be ours   those feelings
nd instead it's your   ive got.
and mine
because we arent   i was raised to be the perfect
together   daughter
and never will be   my mothers feelings came before
                             mine
                                everytime i take a step
hat happens when i loose myself   closer to myself
mpletely   i feel like im
rd we are both wondering why?   betraying myself

                    EATING DISORDER!

it was all my fault   i couldnt be
That you would never   more in awe
  anything to hurt me

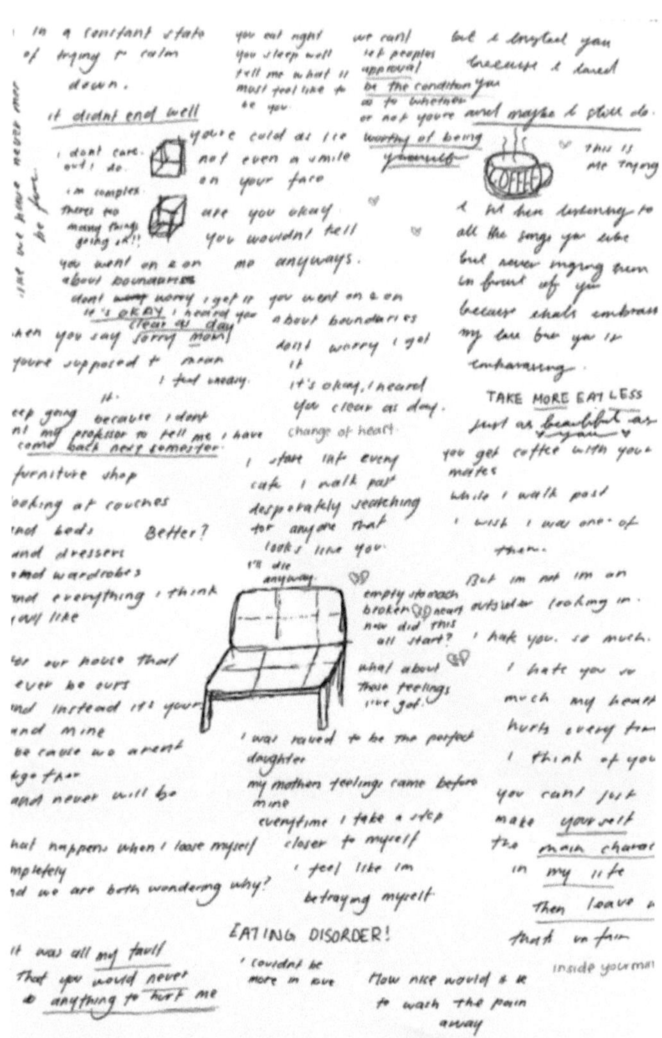

but i trusted you
                because i loved
we cant
let peoples   this is
approval   me trying
be the condition you
as to whether
or not youre   and maybe i still do.
worthy of being
yourself   & i'm been listening to
                    all the songs you like
                    but never singing them
                    in front of you
                    because thats embarrass
                    my love but you is
                    embarrassing.

            TAKE MORE EAT LESS
            just as beautiful as
            you
you get coffee with your
mates
while i walk past
i wish i was one of
    them.

But im not im on
outside looking in.

i hate you so much.

i hate you so
much my heart
hurts every time
i think of you

you cant just
make yourself
the main charac
in my life

    Then leave
that un fair
        inside your mind

How nice would it be
to wash the pain
    away

SLEEPLESS

bare minimum

75

my world revolves around
the people that show me the bare minimum

close

i let you come close,
close enough to hear me breathe,
but not close enough to hear my heart beat
close enough to know my full name,
but not to know my family tree

close enough to touch the surface,
but not enough to drown
within me

i am tired and so are you
of trying to make this dream come true

useless instead of useful

i tied up my hair
after a long day in bed

the night sky fades from blue
to crimson
and then to blue again

i have achieved nothing today

i thought post hospital life would have more
structure
since i am well, right?
i would be more useful

i have a ton of responsibilities
after all i am a daughter,
a sister,
a best friend,
a friend,
and acquaintance

but even with that
i am so useless
and i can never get out of bed

so i am a bad daughter,
a bad sister,
a bad best friend,

a bad friend,
a bad acquaintance,
and a bad person

hush

i don't tell anyone when it hurts
because i know somewhere there is a person
that is in more pain than i am

my mother always told me that
when she had a hard day of work
and my cries were not worth her attention

she told me to quiet down
because she had a headache
and i never cried again

not a single peep
now i am sixteen
i have learned my emotions are not valid

so i carry the guilt
that i might have wasted her time
of all those years
where i used to cry

do not worry mum
it will not happen again
i will be alright

trapped

i stayed in bed all day,
besides those little trips to and from the
bathroom
because i couldn't hold in my pee

i stayed in bed all day,
besides the pit stop to the kitchen to fill up
my bottle to quench my lithium thirst

i stayed in bed all day,
besides the little shimmy to close the blinds
when too much light shines in
and i am blinded by the outside

i stayed in bed all day,
and so has my depression
leaving a me-shaped crease in the sheets,
and an unhealthy weight on my blanket
trapping me

i stayed in bed today,
and yesterday,
and the day before that

*i stayed in bed today,
and will tomorrow,*

and the day after,
and the day after that

anniversary

his anniversary was a few days ago –
I didn't realise it.

it has been about three years,
and it no longer crosses my mind that you
have died.

i thought i would never get over it,
and i thought i would always cry

*but it is three years later i forgot your
anniversary
and it barely crossed my mind*

glue and sticky tape

i am held together by glue and sticky tape to
get through the day,
but it is not the kind you are thinking of

i am held by the exhaustion, the medication,
and the expectation,
to always perform as well as all the other
kids
when i am nowhere near where they are

i am held together by glue and sticky tape to
get through the day,
but you would not know

because for you
it is just another fucking tuesday

sun rises in the summer

i am tired
it is time to go to bed
maybe tomorrow will be better
and the pain will no longer exist
maybe tomorrow a new emotion will arise
and make it better

but for now,
i shall suffer
till the sun rises in the summer

life worth living

I thought about the future,
and cleaned my room
hoping that would jolt that part of my brain
that wants to stay alive

i talk to myself in the mirror only saying
positive things,
because they tell me that it will save my life

I continued to run the race,
because i'm promised a finish line
that is "a life worth living"

10 months have passed
cleaning my room, thinking about the future
hasn't changed my mind,
and i still want to die

10 months have passed
saying positive things in the mirror
hasn't saved my life

10 months have passed
and i no longer believe in a
"life worth living"
and i still want to die

given up on sleep

it is almost one in the morning,
i cannot sleep
dark circles start to form
they have packed their bags and now reside
under my eyes

i persuade myself time and time again
that i do not need meds to knock me out
that i can just naturally sleep
it is almost one in the morning;
take your meds

it is almost two in the morning,
meds have been taken
but no sleep has been achieved
i am getting hot and cold flushes
what is happening to me?

i close my eyes and try to sleep
it is almost two in the morning,
i have not drifted to sleep

it is almost three in the morning,
more tired
but no sleep has been achieved
i toss and turn,

blanket, no blanket,
socks, no socks,
mattress to the floor

*it is almost three in the morning
and i have given up on sleep*

i bet you get told so many things during the
day
the friends and the enemies of friends,
the anger they face,
the depression,
the denial

i bet you see so many people during the day
it is part of your job,
and you do it so well

but i hope you remember me
and my stories,
and my friends and the enemies of my
friends,

the anger i face,
my depression,
my denial

but most of all,
i hope you remember me
as a person,
and nothing else

resemblance

their names don't sound the same,
but the way that they talk you would think
they are twins

their names don't sound the same,
but every time i look at her
i am transported to a room
at two thirty every wednesday

their names don't sound the same,
yet, she has a navy blue car
that is her favourite colour too

their names don't sound the same,
yet, her hair is tied up in a ponytail,
that swings side to side
in the same manner

their names don't sound the same,
but in my mind
i am looking at the same person

take more eat less

i hide the pills in my vitamin bottles
so no one will question my behaviour

i hide the pills that i take in vitamin bottles
so they will not blame my weight loss
on anorexia

i hide the pills that i take in vitamin bottles
to make sure people know i am healthy

you do not get it, it is an addiction
it is my addiction to stop feeling everything
and rather feel nothing besides pain in my
stomach

the pounding in my head that screams
take more, eat less
take more, eat less

take more, eat less
take more
eat less

eternal love

they say some people are only meant to be
loved for a little while
just like your favourite song
or your favourite movie
or your favourite bite to eat

but i hope you are not one of those people
or that favourite song
or that thing you like to eat

i hope i love you for eternity
without breaks,
without distance

*but no matter how close or far apart we
are,
i hope my love always reaches you
and i hope you will always feel it*

life after high school

i cannot help but be envious
of the people around me
whose life after high school
is nothing but a thrilling and freeing
experience

i cannot help but be envious of the plan i
imagined
of myself after walking out those gates
on the last day of school

**i have achieved nothing,
and you, everything**

*it is hard to not compare your life with
someone
when all they got was happiness,
and all you got was misery*

i was raised to be a perfect daughter
that my mothers feelings came before mine
every time i take a step closer to myself
i feel like i am betraying her

crack

you might not know this
or you might pick it up
that i laugh and i smile,
when things get tough

i make people laugh
until they cry
until their stomach hurts
to tell them that no one needs to worry
and there is no need to ask why

but i need you to know
that i overcompensate
how i act
to make sure

that there is never a time
i let my walls down
and you see me crack

so much love

i had so much love for you growing up
looking back now,
it might have been tough for you
who had no sight of love,
healthy love,
stable love,
kind love,
i apologise for loving you too hard
it made you question my intentions

but i want you to know
i love you,
truly

best friend

you were my best friend,
the only person i could count on
but life got in the way,
and i felt betrayed

my emotions got the better of me,
and i went away,
and left you astray

you were my best friend,
but i do not think it
meant anything to you anyway

losing myself

i am starting to lose it again,
overgrown fingernails,
knotted hair,
dry skin,
and eye bags

i am starting to lose it again,
days blending into one
small appetite,
no sleep

i am starting to lose me again
what should i tell my psychiatrist?
will she see through me?

i am starting to lose me again,
what the fuck
pull yourself together,
we cannot go down again

i am starting to lose myself again,
i am so sorry

humiliation

what went through your mind that day
when you humiliated me in front my own
peers
did it make you feel good?
did it boost your ego?
did it make you feel powerful?
you won

because six years later
i still cry at the thought
of your face in that classroom
on the wrong side of line
when you were supposed to be the one
protecting me
instead of teasing me

six years later
i still cry at the thought
that i made myself think i deserved that
when i now know i deserved more than that

i hope this keeps you awake at night
like it does keeps me
i hope you
feel pain over the fact

you pushed me far beyond breaking point
when all i was nothing
but kind to you

where do i put my anger
you tell me to drink a cup of tea
and run a warm bath

but where on earth do i put this anger
do i store it on the kitchen counter
or in the bathroom drawers
or do i store it in the cracks of my bedroom
walls
or even in the school halls

do i store it in the cup of tea
or in the bathtub
or do i store it in me
for the next time someone has the capacity

so put me out of my misery
and tell me
where on earth do i put my anger

mother

"sometimes she would scare me
sometimes she is brutal
she looks like a monster", said
my four year old self,

"but she is still my mother"

daddys little girl

daddys little girl they say
but i lived far away
between cities
him alone in his own house
working hard so i would not have to suffer

i am sorry i do not visit you
and i do not make time for you
but i want you to know
no matter where in the world i live

my heart will always be for you
i will love you just as you love me,
and more

your cup is empty
yet you are still looking
at the same two people
to fill it

MATURE
ENOUGH

mature enough

i was mature
i am mature
i am wise beyond my years

of course i was
i had to keep my family together
even though i was falling apart

i had to keep my family from falling apart
because they did not have the capacity to even try
to keep it together

so i was mature
sitting at the end of the staircase
only being four

peeking through the hole
telling my parents to stop yelling at each other
because i was afraid one of them would get hurt

so i was mature
standing between my two parents
while punches were thrown

in hopes i would take the hit
so they would stop yelling
and that their argument was just for show

so i was mature
clothes thrown on the floor
down the staircase
begging my father
to give my mother another chance
while i watched her pick up her dignity
as she walked out the door

so i was mature
now ten
i was so ready for the relationship
between them to end
because i would rather them
stay friends

so i am mature
i am nineteen
they tell me i am wise beyond my
years

but how do i tell them
that i had to be
so my parents would stop
fighting in front of me

invisible questions

how is treatment?
fine
how are your meds?
fine
are you feeling better?
i do not know
how are you feeling today?
i do not want to live
when is your next therapy appointment?
i stopped going to therapy
have you seen your doctor?
no
full name and date of birth?
you know who i am
what medication are you on?
too many
heard you are back in the hospital, what
happened?
life

any more questions?
no? thank you, finally

comfort

there is comfort in these four walls
there is comfort in being ill
there is comfort in wanting to stay longer
even if it makes you miserable
and there is comfort in being still

there is comfort in being miserable
and there is comfort in isolation
there is comfort in being unstable
and there is comfort in validation

what if one day i wake up
and i don't want to do this anymore?

the night on the bathroom floor

bottles clinking,
vicious raws,
i was in awe
something like this would happen

quiet down
lock the door,
we're safe here for now

silent tears
shaking bodies,
i was scared to death
that i was up next

four hours
felt like twelve
the light at the end was dim

dark room
hard to sleep
paranoid

i never want to do this again

isolation

my isolation has nothing to do with you,
so do not take it personally

my isolation has to do with the universe
not being as kind to me as it was to you

i mean no harm, no damage
i just want rest, from all the misery it gave
me

Mothers Day

they prepare for mothers day
buying gifts and flowers that are just
as beautiful as she is

but mothers day for me
ended ten years ago

when she looked like a monster
more than my mother

anxiety

115

i live in constant anxiety,
no matter what time of the day
i am scared of being alive,
and i am scared of passing away

temporary

close the lid,
time to go,
i was not planning on staying long, you
know

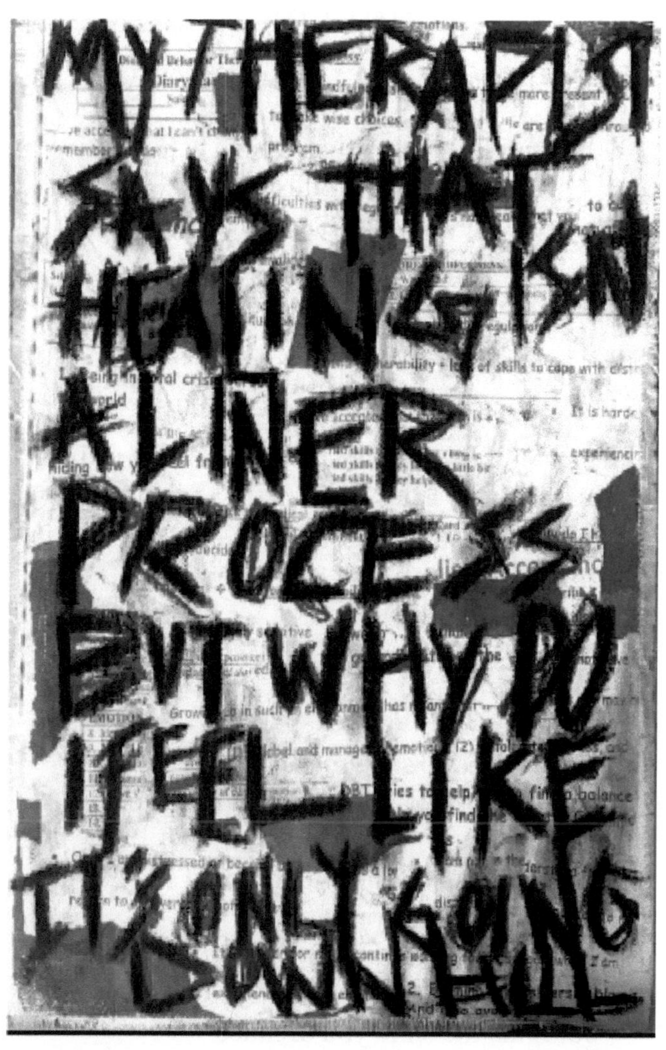
MY THERAPIST
SAYS THAT
HEALING ISN'T
A LINEAR
PROCESS
BUT WHY DO
I FEEL LIKE
IT'S ONLY GOING
DOWNHILL

a little more

the praises and the hugs when i come home
i now should know is bullshit
because they gave up a long ago

because when it became a little more than
depression
when it became a little more than superficial
cat scratches
and a little more than the bullshit that came
out of my mouth
that you told me was not true
and a little more than an overnight hospital
stay
and a little more than *that is the devil
talking they say*

you decided to send me away
because you did not want to damage our
family name
and when it became long hospital stays,
abuse of medication,
loss of appetite,
suddenly i was not the child you wanted
but i was the child you dreaded

and that is fine by me
but do not walk in on my appointments
and tell my therapist,
my psychiatrists,
and my nurses,

that you love me
and would do anything for me
because that is not true,
and we both know that

do not come into my appointments
and cry, begging me to stay
when all you wanted me to do is die

because when the time comes
and i am discharged and come back home
that smile turns into a frown
and i am no longer welcomed in your house

as soon as i step into the front door of your
house
that love is no longer there
or anywhere in this household

*because you left it in the hospital
eighteen years ago*

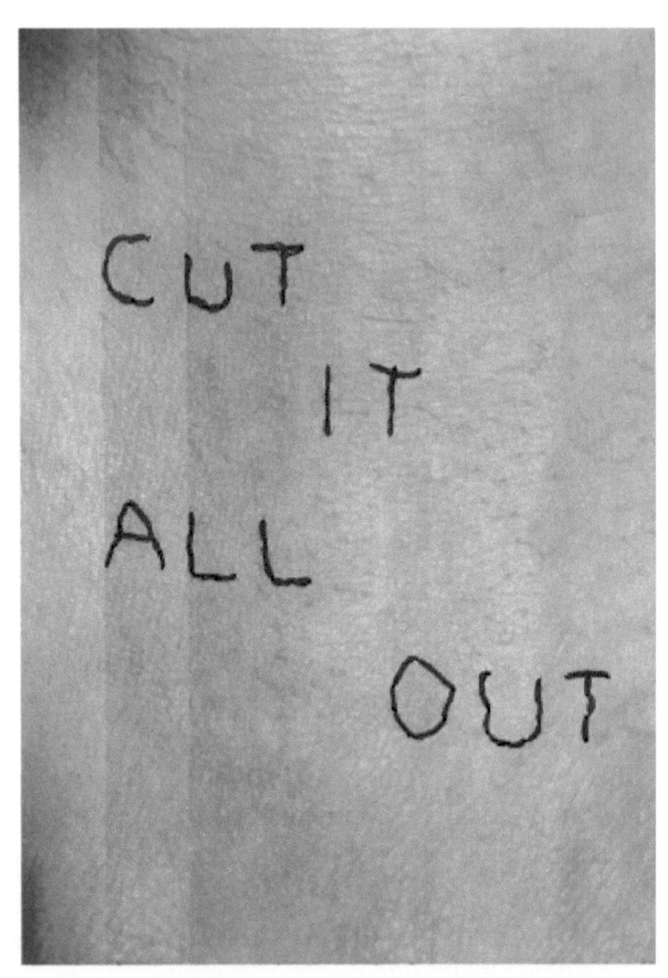
CUT
IT
ALL
OUT

music loud to drown out
the thoughts

roar

i finally got them
no need to lie anymore
it hurt the people around me
and it made them want to go away
but now they will listen

because it is no longer a scream,
it is a fucking roar

we cannot let other people's approval
be the condition
as to whether or not
we are worthy of being ourselves
-M

struggle

abusing my meds
when life is tough
and one tablet is not enough
to make me sleep for a week

*nothing to worry about
i have done this for weeks*

relief

home for me was more people
than places
as i moved around

i found homes in everywhere i went
and sometimes
when it gets too much
and i need to go to bed
i would have a house waiting for me

what a relief
that i have you guys
what a relief, we are together

day ahead

eye bags
i cover with concealer
for the new day ahead

bruises
i cover with band-aids
so no one will ask
no one would question

all the torture i endured
the night before
and all the preparation
for the day ahead

quite some time

i am sorry that i missed your call
i am sorry i do not go outside
i have been unwell for quite some time

i am sorry i hide
when things come to my mind

i have been unwell for quite some time

red marks

she was lost
so she came to me
asking for the brush
that i used

*to paint red marks
on her dear wrist*

body

i look at myself,
hate what i see
ruined my body
but at the end of the fucking day,
i am still me

t.w

you should not have let me walk out the
door
cause after that i put a knife to my wrist
and sat there with blood on the floor

i am floating
and nobody understands
how it feels to constantly stay afloat

downhill

i am starting to go downhill
so i skip meals,
stay home,
because i would rather be alone

talking to the walls and ceilings
rather than talk about my feelings
i would stay sleeping
instead of healing

pushing down how i feel
because i was taught that my feelings are
not real

how nice would it be
to just wash the pain
away

shivers, tremors and chatters

my whole body aches
i had the shivers,
the tremors,
the chatters,

it's been a week since i stopped taking my
meds
now i am here
unwell
and still wanting to die

my whole body aches
i had the shivers,
the tremors,
the chatters

was this all worth it for a little bit of sanity
was this all worth it for a little bit of a cry

save me

avoidance,
it is something i do
when things are tough

it is more to prepare those around me
for the worst to come
a final goodbye to planet earth
so when i do reach my breaking point
and end it

people do not hate themselves
for not trying hard enough
to save me

thorns and shadows

the night sky,
i used to look at it a lot
while taking a deep breath

filling my lungs with the polluted air
but it was comforting you see
seeing other peoples thorns
be lit by the moon

but i had to stop,
i could not make my eyes meet it
the view reminded me of my past
so i too decided to leave it

but today i come back,
filling my lungs with the same air
i spread my arms out like before

i close my eyes,
and i make peace with the past
honouring my thorns and shadows

as it is a part of me
it is a part of who i am

this is me trying

i try,
i try to wake up in the morning
instead of staying asleep in bed

i try to be productive,
reading books, checking emails
doing things most adults do
i try and stay on task so i do not fall behind
but then i start to cry

it is too difficult you see
doing all these things
what about me?
what about how i feel?

i am losing myself
in each book
each email i respond to,
each task i finish

by the time i am done with everything
i am no longer me,
but instead a reflection of society
and how it has changed me

i do not know who i am anymore

and i am too tired to find out
so let me just blend in
and it will be alright

at least for now

i feel so misunderstood

139

mother pt2

her words were rough
but she grew up tough
she meant nothing but kindness
but it all came out wrong

i know she did not mean it
and only wanted the best

i am blessed
to call her my mother

toss and turn

today has been harder than usual
simple tasks are overwhelming

so i stayed in bed,
tossing and turning,
hoping with each toss and each turn
that the part of me that hates the idea of
staying alive would lessen
a little bit
but it does not

so i lie here,
tears streaming down my face

i am sorry
i don't want to be here anymore

i sit here and mourn you
but to be honest
i have no idea what i am mourning

battles

i see you,
beyond your facade,
beyond your intelligence,
and big words,

beyond your titles
i see the pain and suffering,
even the ones you do not mention
i see you in a different light,
compared to how they see you

and maybe there is much i do not know
the secret internal battles you are fighting
but i want to let you know

that i love you more than love
and i hope your trials end in ease
because you deserve nothing less than that

do not come back

you do not get to come back
and act like you did not traumatise me that
night
you do not get to come here
and act like you did not do anything

just because you were in more pain than i
was in that night
you were drunk and on drugs,
that is the choice you made

you brought fear to a place
that was to be safe
i was deserving of a safe environment,
but i did not get that

you were not a victim that night;
you were the perpetrator,
the bad guy,
the scary monster under my bed

and you should live with that,
you shall rot with that
do not ever think of ever coming back

D

all those days
turned into months
then years,
then four,
all that time,
did you ever look for me?

hoping you see me again
all that time did you ever cry,
did your heart ever ache?

did you avoid the things we used to do?
the things we used to eat,
the places we used to go,
or did you revisit all those things,
in hopes you would accidentally see me?

four years went by
since we last saw each other
and it was the shortest
yet the longest time in my life

*but you are here now
reunited in my arms
and i thank god every day,
you are here to stay*

walked out

that night,
i was miserable
like i lost a whole chunk of my identity
because you walked out

and i hated myself
wishing i would just drop dead
so i would not have to live a life
without you in it

i tried many ways
to get you back
because i could not function without you
because you had an impact
on my teenage years

but i could not deal with it,
and i have never wanted to disappear more
than i wanted to that night

you kissed me on the forehead
and said goodnight
tucked teddy in
and said every thing will be alright

you left my room
without a sound
and when i woke up
you were no where to be found

you spend your days
not at home
i always wonder
where you roam

please tell me you are
alright
so i dont worry every night

i am in a constant state of trying to calm
down

In complete

I walk away
from every conversion
needing to change something
about myself
because being me
is not enough for anyone

So I walk away
from every conversation
losing a piece of me
until I am nothing
but all my faults and shortcomings

It is my fault
that the world
spins the wrong way
and it is my fault
that the sun rises
in the west and sets in the east

and it is my fault
I am incomplete

dictation

i do not think you know how serious this is
you do not see the tears,
or the times i struggle to get out of bed

or the paralysis my body goes through,
or all the voices in my head,
or the times i struggle to ask for help

you only see how i bounce back
with my fashionable clothes
from head to toe,
and precise make up

so do not go telling me how to feel,
do not go telling me how to feel
when you have only seen me at my best

and never at my worst
so do not make assumptions on how you
think my life is
when you only see one quarter of it

you do not get to hush me,
you do not get to hush me
because i do not fit your stereotype
and you do not get to hush me

just cause you think i am fine

since when was this about you?
since when do you get to dictate how i feel
and what is real
in my life?

so take five steps back,
because you only know me a little bit,
or maybe you do not know me at all

youre deceptive, like youre polite with your sadness. she pauses
'feel like i have missed something, have we missed something
? you look smiley and you dress well, i feel like we have mise
d something with you. i think im lying to myself. am i?
i was unmedicated for so long i have learnt how to deal
with things the hard way. no one really took me seriously
the panic attacks ~~at age 11~~ in your 11 and the suicidal
urges at age 11. everything i was doing was overlooked
or unacknowledge. am i lying to myself when they asked
if i struggle with daily tasks like hygiene. now that i think
about it, brush [Liar] [Liar pants on fire] such a hassle
but fixed with [ ] air tie. am i
lying to myself [ ] ating at school
you do very well. your grades are exceptional. youre
highly intelligent young lady theres no adhd there. but
there is. all day everyday, and god fucking damn it.
it's always a struggle. am i lying to myself when those
ask me to do a presentation in front of the class, or
stand infront of an audience to battle for first place
in a national speech contest at the age of fourteen
four years later.... im eighteen now and im scared to
pick up the phone.

trial and ease

154

i have been numb
i have been in pain for half of my life

it is a risk to continue
when nothing is promised

so why do you live?
when it is easier to die

when there is trial
there is ease

so where is mine?

what do you do
when every day is another struggle?
what do you do
when you are thrown in the deep end
and no one is there to save you?
suddenly, drowning might be the best way
out
suddenly, death seems comforting

R

you went through so much
from having a terrible childhood
to fucked up parents

i watched as you slowly lose yourself
in each page of that textbook
your eyes were fixated on
for the past fifteen hours

i watched you lose yourself
in those classrooms
that held you captive

but i thought if i loved you hard enough,
life would be easier for you
and i thought if i gathered all those pieces
up,
i would see the you that i know

but you were long gone,
i could not save you

and i could not live with that,
so i hope you learn to live with the new you
because i am sorry i could not

answers

what do i tell my professor
when it is starting to get bad again and i
cannot finish my assignments?
what do i tell my therapist
when i have run out of coping skills?
what do i tell my psychiatrist
when my meds are inconsistent?
what do i tell my parents
when i no longer want to live in this world?
what do i tell my friends
when they will never see me again?

i don't feel good,
i feel like throwing up

cold winter day

i bet you would not be able to recognise me
if you walked past

i changed my hair
and the way i look

washing off,
everything that you had on me
i am free from you

*i am no longer the person you met
on that cold winter day*

eating disorder

i have lost it,
it is the 4th day
that i have lost
to my eating disorder brain

sobs in each room of the house,
to the hearts that i have broken
the exhausted faces
"eat please"
a phrase i have heard for years
and a phrase i hoped to never hear again

i could not look at them in the same way
i hurt them
" you do not care about us"
"you do not love us"
"its easier to look after animals"

i stand there with my hood up
head in my hands
as the door slams

i begged the universe to swallow me whole
i would not have to deal with this if i was dead
after all of this would be better unsaid

i don't tell them why
i take the long way
i don't tell them why
i would rather walk home in the rain

and i don't tell them why
i choose skim milk over normal milk

and i don't tell them that
i have not eaten when they offer me food

or that i spend hours in the grocery store
but only to come out with burnt calories
and nothing more
cause they do not need to know these secrets

they don't need to know my weakness
or that i am more scared of food than bungee
jumping

that is not for them to know
and all i get from it is control

secrecy

you hid me like i was some kind of secret,
like something you should be ashamed of
for all these years i thought it was me,
that i was the person you regretted
but no, it was all you

and your secrets,
and your stupid mind games,
and everyone you blamed,
and the dirty hands you refused to wipe
clean,
and all the bloody crime scenes

hands up, you are caught –
i got you,
you liar

how could you keep it from me?
i do not know who you are
which is funny

because i should know you,
i should know every part of you
i am your girl after all,
but you made me feel so small

the city

the city does not want you here
it is time to go
it is time to say goodbye
and let go

they are pretty,
and they are soft and caring
they are kind,
and they make me smile
although i have not known them for a while
it has felt like forever
and i do not know what all this means

i am not very good with this,
but i think i like you

drowning

i think i am drowning
but i would not be able to tell you
i do not know myself enough
to entirely understand what is happening
in this chaotic mind of mine
i think i am   drowning
but i would not   be able to
tell   you
because   it has been
too   long
for me to tell   the difference
between   drowning
under   water
and drowning   at surface

l e   v e l

it did not end well

i was so hung up over you,
i walked past your work
every day hoping i would see you,
and i would get the closure i needed
that you could not give me

searching you up on the internet,
desperate
trying to find a way
to forget about you

but at the end of the day,
all fails
and i am the one hurting again

i spent hours sitting there on the bench
hail, rain or shine,
just to possibly get a glimpse of you
do you not see it?
is this not obvious?

i stay looking
through every single person
in hopes that in one of those million people,
you are there

one conversation
one smile or wave
or acknowledgment

that i exist to you
more than a case file

you disappoint me,
but i disappoint myself

that after a year
i have not been able to let go
and that is how it is going to be for now

i am exhausted from talking
i no longer care about validation,
but rather isolation
from the world around me

i cannot sleep early
i am used to crying myself to sleep
or hearing my mum cry
after the fight
i wish i never started

sorry to the people i love,
it was not supposed to end like this
but i will keep trying until i succeed
and death will comfort me indeed

i don't feel heard
because i still hear voices
of those who have failed me

saying that you will never hurt deep enough
for someone to listen to you

this is not enough
this damage is not enough

and you know they are wrong
but you will never win

because you are so consumed
by what they think

i am sorry i was not the person you needed;
i exhausted myself

things have gotten worse
since we last spoke

i wish it was a joke
it is just i have been empty
and ignoring the signs
even when i feel like my body is burning out
all i can say is that i am fine

i have not been sleeping
or eating
okay yeah, maybe it is as worse as you think

i try,
i try and i try,
even when all it makes me want to do is cry

i want you to know
things have gotten worse
since we last spoke
and my body is burning out

it is kind of complicated though
because
it never stopped raining on my side of town

recovery?

i don't think i was ever able to recover
i spent a year
picking up all the pieces
of myself because of my mother

only to fall back in an instant
which makes me wonder
if i ever was recovered at all

or was i pretending to try my hardest
so people wouldn't be disappointed in me

or did the hours of therapy
persuade me
that i was okay even though i wasn't
all those coping skills
countless hours of praying
to whoever was up there

did that mean nothing
if in the first place
i never wanted to get better
at all

this is not me
	who is this?
		the familiar feeling
		is gone
	am i getting better?
		is this what it is?

		how come
i do not deserve this
		i am supposed to suffer
i am supposed to ache
				paying for the sins of the
						dead

it feels stupid
			because once i wanted this
					to END
i wanted the pain to stop
but the only way to stop it
							is to stop
			my heart too

i was supposed to
						die
so why am i
			given things to live for

is this what they call

A LIFE WORTH LIVING?

now i am learning
        to live a
                life
a life i never wanted to
                   live
a fate i never wanted to be true
this is the calm before
                       the storm
im forgetting where i am
              from
                  please get me out
of here

i need to be wronged
                by those who
are right

i was supposed to
                       die
from the
           fight
          BUT NOW I AM ALIVE
                    & afraid
of the
           light
and how it shines
           in my eyes

i will learn how to
                SWIM
            but rather
            D
              R
                O
                  W
                    N

        in the abyss
                of this

TOWN

this is the END
i am not
            going to
        PRETEND
                that once
i wanted to be FREE

                        now all of this
    is scaring

                ME;

my life is full of regrets
and continuing on is one of them

I started off with something funny
but Im not laughing. I wrote a couple
of pages of poetry and random
thoughts to kinda settle. because this
is becoming a little dangerous.

i have been thinking about this for
a while now. Im probably going to
deactivate my account. so you
have my number, you have my
whatsapp. so probably text
me over there. cause um... i
need a break for a bit.
dont worry though. im okay
i love you.
good night.

180622 - afterward

to whoever is willing to listen,

for the past seven years of my life i have suffered multiple debilitating mental disorders that have made daily tasks nearly impossible to complete. but alongside this tiredness, i have this perfectionist voice in my head that strives to be the best in every single thing i do. and now as i have gotten older, i have realised how unfair that expectation of me to be the best 24/7 is when i am fighting to get up in the morning. ***so why is it that you haven't been able to notice?***

i kept the internal battles quiet until it started to become visible in my actions and behaviours. i was told to seek help because it will make me feel better, but for most of my life i declined it, fearing invalidation or comments like "you are crazy", or that i am asking for attention. but finally, i decided to reach out to people, in the hopes they would treat me how they promised to. but unfortunately, that never happened. every single therapist, counsellor, and support officer i have gone to has treated me like shit. *and no, I did not feel better like they said i would.*

and they say something along the lines of ***"we see you", "we hear you", "you are valid",*** *then they turn a blind eye on the girl on the bathroom floor with a blade to her wrist.*

i constantly challenge that thought and tell myself i am worth working on. but every new person i go to proves that thought wrong. they say ***"no, you are not worth working on and you never will be".***

"stay alive", they say, *"so we can help you".* when have you fucking helped me? name a time you saw my fresh scars and asked if i was okay. name a time you saw my fresh scars and did something. *you offered to send me home, how is that a fix to what happened?*

just because it did not happen under your supervision, it does not mean you are not responsible for what led me to go through it.

and i am not quiet about my mental health now. i make it obvious that i am struggling, but i seem to think we are both speaking different languages, **because time and time again, you have failed to see the signs.**

i do not want you to send me home with a safety plan, i do not want you to send me home with a long list of symptoms of low blood sugar levels.

i want you to listen when i am talking to you, not just do the bare minimum, and maybe if you are not fit for the job then do not waste time making me believe something that i am not.

i am hurting and it is pretty visib. i do not know how else to make you believe i am struggling. should i hurt myself more? abuse my meds or just fucking step in front of a train? will you finally believe i hurt too, i hurt every single damn day, every single second of the day? **because i am determined to show the world how painful it is in my shoes, even if it means i do not wake up in the morning.**

because when the time comes that blood no longer trickles down my arms, it is on you. when the time comes when i successfully cut myself into tiny little pieces, you will live with the guilt that no, you did not try hard enough. you treated me like a burden on your long list of things to do. you are the ones that did not believe the cries and screams for help, you are the ones that took my future away, ruined my chances of living a healthy life and you were the ones that brought my parents crying to their knees.

at the end of the day, i did not kill myself, you did.
you killed me

Acknowledgements

First, I would like to thank the ones that broke my heart, yes, you. Without the pain, I would not have been able to create something great from it; Heartbreak and Sleepless nights would not exist.

I would like to extend my deepest gratitude to my editor and one of my closest friends Miss Ramla Khalid. Thank you for all your hard work and patience when working with me. Heartbreak and Sleepless nights is your project just as much as it is mine. I am forever grateful for all your help with this project. Thank you again.

To my illustrator and my second editor Miss Claudia Jackson, you are amazing. Thank you for turning my little doodles into the most amazing pieces of art I have ever seen; it truly makes this book look more alive. Thank you for supporting me from day one and liking my posts on Tumblr. I am so grateful that you agreed to this project. I would not have wanted anyone else doing illustrations than you. You have my love.

To my inner circle, Peaches, Marcel, D and Mutiara, thank you for keeping me alive. Thank you for always being there for me and supporting me in all aspects of my life. What would I do without you all.

To my girl Raisa, you have always been an inspiration to me, I admire you so much. Thank you for always sticking by my side even though we are miles apart.

To my ward family, Amy, Tori, and everyone else. Where do I start, thank you for also keeping me alive. Thank you for being supportive and believing in my skills to turn this from an ordinary Tumblr blog to my first self-published poetry book. Thank you for inspiring me to write and share my talent. You know who you are. I love you more than love.

To Noah, thank you for sticking by my side through the last stages of publishing. Thank you for always supporting me and encouraging me to do my best.

To my Tumblr followers, thank you for loving my poems. Thank you for always being there with your kind comments, reblogs and likes. Big love to my og family<3

To M... thank you, for everything, for all the little everythings. It all started with you telling me to journal and self-reflect, now I have my own published poetry book. Thank you for always encouraging me to achieve my goals, I hope you are proud of me.

To my senior English teacher Ms Melinda Wells, thank you for letting me hide out in your classroom, and inspiring my creativity. Thanks for always supporting me through my hardest times during high school. I genuinely would not be alive today without you. I love you<3

To Ms Ati and Ms Mima, I would like to take the time to thank you both for your immense support in my life, from when I was a preteen to now as an adult. You both inspire me in many ways, and I am grateful for your existence in my life. Makasih ya sudah sayang sama Rani, aku cinta kalian.

To the cheerleader in my life, you know who you are. Thank you for taking the time to read my draft manuscript, even though you did not have to. Thank you for taking the time to understand me through my poetry. Thank you for giving me a reason to stay alive. Even though our relationship was short lived, shorter than we expected, I am grateful that I was able to share my work with you. Wherever you are reading this right now, I want you to know that I appreciate you always. Take care:)

To my family, thank you for raising me, I love you very much. Thank you for supporting me through all the hardships that I have endured in my life. Sprouts, you are included in this too. Thank you for being the best writing partner I could ever have. Thank you for staying up with me and comforting me when I get frustrated and start to cry.

Last but certainly not least, I would like to thank Gloria and Book Leaf Publishing, for being extremely patient with me during the writing and publishing process. Without you guys, my dream would not have come true. You have my deepest appreciation.

Socials

187

Tumblr: @cantsleephomesick
Instagram: heartbreakandsleeplessnights_
Tiktok: @cantsleephomesick

Resources

"people who seek help are deserving of it"

Beyond Blue
Beyondblue.org.au
1300 22 4636

Black Dog Institute
Blackdoginstitue.org.au

Headspace
Headspace.org.au
1800 650 890

Headtohealth
Headtohealth.gov.au
1800 595 212

Kids helpline
Kidshelpline.com.au
1800 55 1800

Lifeline
Lifeline.org.au
13 11 14

Mensline
Mensline.org.au
1300 78 99 78

One Door
onedoor.org.au
1800 843 539

SANE Help
www.sane.org
1800 187 263

Suicide call back service
Suicidecalbackservice.org.au
1300 659 467

13 YARN
www.13yarn.com.au
13 92 76

Printed by Libri Plureos GmbH in Hamburg, Germany